T0198756

Living Life Through
Angel's Eyes

SUE LEHMAN

i

AuthorHouse™
1663 Liberty Drive
Bloomington, IN 47403
www.authorhouse.com
Phone: 1 (800) 839-8640

Because of the dynamic nature of the Internet, any web addresses or links contained in this book may have changed
since publication and may no longer be valid. The views expressed in this work are solely those of the author and do
not necessarily reflect the views of the publisher, and the publisher hereby disclaims any responsibility for them.

Any people depicted in stock imagery provided by Getty Images are models,
and such images are being used for illustrative purposes only.
Certain stock imagery © Getty Images.

This book is printed on acid-free paper.

ISBN: 978-1-7283-3717-3 (sc)
ISBN: 978-1-7283-3719-7 (hc)
ISBN: 978-1-7283-3718-0 (e)

Print information available on the last page.

Published by AuthorHouse 11/27/2019

authorHOUSE®

Dedication

In Loving Memory of Paradise Angel Wings,
our dearest boxer dog. Gone too soon, but never Forgotten!
Nov.24,2009 – Feb.2,2019

Sometimes when you're feeling sad, when all you want is me,
I softly sit and gently put my head upon your knee,
Some nights when your heart does ache, worn out by the tears you weep,
I quietly lie beside your bed and guard you as you sleep.
Somewhere far beyond this place,
A land where all run free,
I'm calmly watching over you,
And waiting patiently.
Someday when the time is right,
Your voice will call to me,
And I'll come running like the wind,
Someday…wait and see

Table of Contents

Chapter 1
Finding my way Home

The search was on, the search for a new puppy that is! David Helmuth had a wonderful male boxer dog named Jackson, for short we often called him Jack. Jackson lived with Dad (David), he was looking for another puppy as a companion and gift to his girlfriend. David was very strategic in his search for a new puppy it had to meet specific criteria. He wanted to have me to look like his beautiful horses, with a brindle color and white socks. After days of searching through 1243 puppy profiles on puppy find.com, he finally narrowed it down to only -one which was me!! I was born and raised in New York City. I was sad to leave my family, but very excited to meet my new Daddy. He paid for my airfare so that I could be flown all the way to Georgia. This was an incredible flight. I was so grateful to finally arrive and to be greeted with such a warm welcome from my new Daddy -David Helmuth. I had so many little puppy kisses saved up just for him! On our drive from the airport back to my new home, I had completely licked him from head to toe. It was such a comfort to snuggle with him as my new security. I guess I was actually supposed to be his girlfriend's dog but I really didn't care for her. He would hand me over, so that she could hold me. I jumped and scrambled, soon I was back on his lap, Wow- what a view, from the driver's seat, as we drove down the road with the big semi! I knew that Dad personally handpicked me so I wanted to be extremely loyal to him, although I never fully felt at ease with her.

For a while I was completely in my glorious element, I got to go home with Daddy and his girlfriend, I was Queen of the house. Unfortunately, that didn't last long soon their relationship was dissolved. I was a gift for her now, I was forced to go with her to now live at her house in

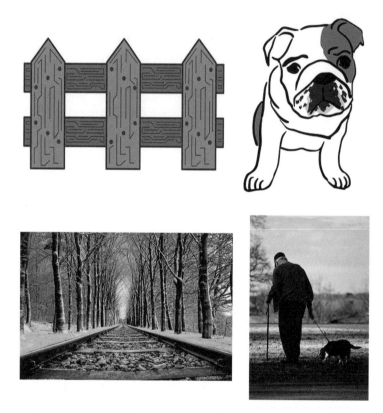

Florida. It didn't take me long and I had formulated a plan. I decided when she is at work, I am going to see how fast my paws can dig. This was something that I hadn't ever done before. I was always sweet and well-mannered for Daddy because I had no reason to do anything else. Now my only mission was to get back to my dear Daddy. As soon as she left to go to work, I was on my way. I was penned in the back yard, so I started digging my way out. Wow, that wasn't as hard as I thought, I was out and headed NORTH. My goal was to get to DADDY! All I knew we were south in Florida and I needed to go north to Georgia. I made it to the railroad, it looked like the perfect path for me. My enthusiasm was soon turned to disappointment!! A very mean looking man with a net was running after me… I guess you call him a dog catcher. He called the number on my collar and sure enough, I was taken back home. Much to my despair, my perfectly formulated plan got ruined. She kept me pinned in the house so, I had to come up with another idea. I decided my only option was to jump out of the upstairs window. I waited until the time was right, as I busted through the 2nd story window, breaking the screen and glass. Boom!!! I landed on the ground many feet below. When I got my wits together after the fall, I jumped up and headed north once more. I was feeling accomplished, as I once again reached the train tracts in Mt. Dora, Fl. Although, it seemed as though the dog catcher knew that I was on the run once more. He caught me again at about the same spot, and carried back to my momma. This time he had a very in-depth conversation with her, telling her that if he catches me again, I won't be coming home. This really worried her, so she called Daddy. She told David you better come to get your dumb dog! Dad was completely appalled; he couldn't believe that I was acting out. Furthermore, he was shocked that she wanted to give me back, since I was her gift. Although I was beyond excited, I finally got to go back to my Daddy!!

Chapter 2

Living with my Hero – Jack

I was so happy
and content!

At home with
Daddy and Jack.

We had very important
roles to fulfill!

Jack was a brilliant
example for me, he
thought I was just
a silly puppy, but
he was my hero!
I knew Daddy was
extremely proud of
Jack, so I wanted
to be just like him!

It didn't take long and I started to realize, Jack needed more and more sleep. Daddy said, I need to take it easy on him because he isn't feeling well lately! This made me very sad, because I didn't want to lose my playmate. Yet I wanted to take good care of Jack because I really loved him! As the days grew into months, we understood Jack had a horrible disease called cancer. We knew Jack's spirit wanted to always be with us, although his physical body was wearing out. I decided I'm going to make the most of our time together, before he goes home to puppy land!

This picture represents one of my best ever Christmas', it was my last Christmas with my big buddy Jack.

As Jack started fading, I had to grow up fast, because it was important for me to help out Daddy with the horses and all that entailed.

Daddy's magnificent boys (horses) needed me to watch over them at times. I took my job very seriously, but most of all I loved racing with them out in the open meadows. Sometimes the boys got a little upset with me, because I was always the winner of our races!

Daddy's job for eighteen years, consisted of traveling all over the United States, doing parades and other special events. We loaded the horses and stagecoach into a BIG semi and traveled in first class from city to city! During the events Jack and I rode on top of the stagecoach. This picture shows Jack was a perfect mascot, he sat on top as he greeted everyone down below! Jack made it look so simple, so I decided I'll be brave and give it a shot. Wow, it was completely different than I expected!! The stagecoach is tall and the ground below looked far away. It probably wouldn't have been so bad if I just laid down like Jack did. I was too curious, before I knew it I had fallen off the back side during a parade! Yikes, that was scary! Thankfully Dad was always prepared for the worst, he had my leash tied on top of the stagecoach so I didn't completely fall off. Also, as always Dad had crew members walking on each side of the stagecoach, so they could alert him to any dangers below. The crew member, Nick, saw me topple down and immediately scooped me up and put me back on top. No worries, I wasn't ever going to try that again!

The time came that we had to put Jack down, removing him from his painful misery of esophageal cancer. If it would have helped I would've posted these wanted pictures all over town, but Daddy said it's time for Jack to move on and go to doggy heaven. Now at home all we have left are his ashes in a box and lots of magnificent memories.

Six months after your dog passes you still can't bear to talk about her. Yet, some may say "She was just a dog."

You reach under the bed and stumble across an old toy of hers and burst into tears. Yet, she was just a dog.

After a long and mentally draining day at work, you'd give anything to come home and just cuddle with her. Yet, she was just a dog.

Those who never owned one, will never get it. That dog was your friend, cuddle buddy, jogging partner, playmate, anxiety reliever, guard dog, alarm clock, etc.....

Just a dog, right?

Paradise Angel wnigs

Rest in PEACE Sir Jackson

Chapter 3

Rising to fill the Position

I was growing up fast and determined to prove to Dad that I could take on where Jack had left off. I knew that Dad was sad that Jack was no longer with us. I made it my mission to restore my Dad's happiness, after all he had saved my life. Dad understood my need to help out, he started entrusting me with major duties when we were on the road doing all the events. The day Dad put me in charge of the horses, I knew I had won his trust!

In Complete
Control…

A photo taken by one of Angels' Greatest fans.

Chapter 4

Greeting the crowd, Serving – Proud

We were on the road more than we were at home, but I didn't care I was happy where ever we went!

I no longer needed a leash, I was always in Daddy's sights. I had no reason to run, I was right where I wanted to be!

I was the luckiest dog in the world!

MERRY CHRISTMAS, ST. PATTY'S DAY, it didn't matter what the occasion was; we did it All! We were the most dependable crew around, never late and without complaint. Rain, sleet, snow, or hail we kept on going to prevail.

Spreading Cheer both Far and Near..

They called me Famous "Angel", must be because I've been EVERYWHERE...

We were meeting celebrities on a daily basis, as we traversed throughout.

Washington D.C. Memorial Day Parade, Indy 500 Parade, Kentucky Derby Pegasus Parade, Rose Bowl Parade,and so many more on multiple occasions!

Chapter 5

Comforting Dad

Dad and I completely understood each other, there were times when he was alone so really all he had at the time was me. I would do my best to understand, love, and comfort him all through the thick and the thin! Through the years I had two litters of puppies. I was able to give a little back to him, for all he had done for me! My Puppies were always in great demand from all of my fans along the way.

Sometimes he even needed me to drive, while other times I only needed to go along for the ride.

On the rare occasion that we were at home we enjoyed our time off together. One of my favorite hobbies was to go out on the boat, lucky for me; Dad equally enjoyed the water!

Chapter 6

Moving On

Dad and I were in sync with each other, I could sense when he needed help and comfort. In 2018 our world was dramatically changed, on various levels, we were moving on to new horizons. Dad bought our very own one- of a kind authentic and completely refurbished stagecoach. We were no longer a part of another company; we had completely stepped out on our own! This was rather exciting, now we could pick and choose which events that we wished to grace with our presence. Dad decided to take the year off and let the horses run free in the pastures. Meanwhile the calendar was filling up fast with events for 2019. In January we were ready to roll, into our new adventure. We had a new semi, new stagecoach and most importantly a new crew! During our whole transition Dad's only human daughter, Sue Ann and her three children, Heather, Wyatt, and Jennifer joined our team! Our first show after the break, was set to be the Grandview Invitational at the Florida Horse Park in Ocala, Fl. This worked out perfectly, because through it all, we had also acquired a new property in Ocala. The 3-day event was basically in our new neighborhood!

THE HISTORIC STAGE COACH TEAM

Angel was super excited and thoroughly enjoyed filling her position atop the stagecoach once more! We were honored to have Angel with us to debut our brand-new adventure as we are now The Historic Stage Coach Team! Unbeknownst to us Angel had just ridden her last ride....

2010-2019

In loving memory of our dear dog, Angel

On the last evening of the show, Angel was beyond herself, as she was jumping all over us in an extra exuberant manner. It was as if she was telling us she will no longer be with us. Angel was so full of life so we were completely shocked to find out the next morning that Angel had passed on…

Angel will always know how it all went down, but to us it remains a bizarre mystery???? Angel was not ready to die! Sometimes in life a Angel will die for her Daddy, so he can be spared- because "they" want no one else spared.

- More to be reveled in a coming book-

Our Dear, Paradise Angel Wings gave her all, in all she did,
Now she rests blissfully at the Ocala Ranch.
A tribute to the BEST boxer in the world... you were a gift from
God! We miss you Angel and will Always Love You,
Dad and the Crew

Angel's Memories

Angel always loved to go for a ride

Chapter 7
Introducing Baby Angel

Over six months had passed since we buried Paradise Angel Wings. We will never forget her. Although in life we must go on, so we started looking for Angel II. As we browsed numerous sites online we couldn't find the perfect puppy. We made a commitment to one puppy, but when the time came to pick her up somehow it just didn't feel right. We passed on that puppy and allowed her to go onto another loving home. A couple of months later we finally did find another little puppy, that we felt could suit our needs. We drove from Marion Co. Florida to Marion Co. South Carolina, to pick up our newest addition to the team. We named this puppy Angel Rose, as a tribute to Paradise Angel Wings. We brought her home and immediately she became part of us!

Jennifer and Angel are going for a potty break at the rest area , on the first trip home.

Angel II first newborn baby picture

Angel II has got this!

The first car ride back home

Wyatt sharing his seat

Chapter 8

Bright Futures Ahead

Angel II is growing fast, and adapting very well to her new family and surroundings. There is so much to be seen and done on the Helmuth Ranch! Angel II makes it her mission to keep up with all the activities. She is always tuckered out by the end of the day. As she watches Heather- feed the boys (horses), runs to chase after Jennifer as she rides her bike, playing fetch with Wyatt, and so much more.

One morning before Daddy had to leave he was singing a song to Angel in the office. Singing- "Angel girl you don't do nothing, you can't even catch a squirrel." It was all in fun, but seemingly she took it as a challenge. We were completely amazed the very next time as we went outside she presented to us, her prize as pictured above.

She was extremely proud of herself as she tackled and ate the squirrel.

Angel II is becoming a very smart girl, as she proudly fulfills the duties of being our family dog at the Helmuth Ranch!

We are all looking forward to many more Precious memories to be made together!

-Angel II and the Crew

A bundle of sweetness.

Angel always enjoys riding along to and from school. She is pictured here as she anticipates the children's arrival to the truck to head back home.

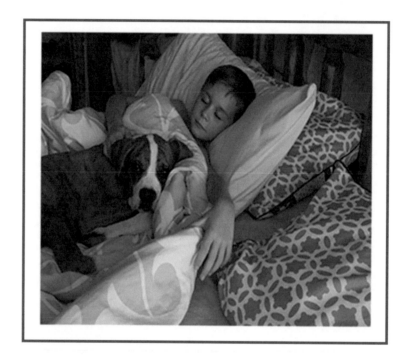

Angel snuggling with Wyatt as he sleeps.

Angel loving the boat rides.

Angel won't be a puppy for long, she is growing up fast!

Heather holding Angel on the ride home from school.

Angel found the perfect hiding spot, she loves digging in the sand.

Angel is always eager and readily waiting for the next command.

🐾 Color Page 🐾

Printed in the United States
By Bookmasters